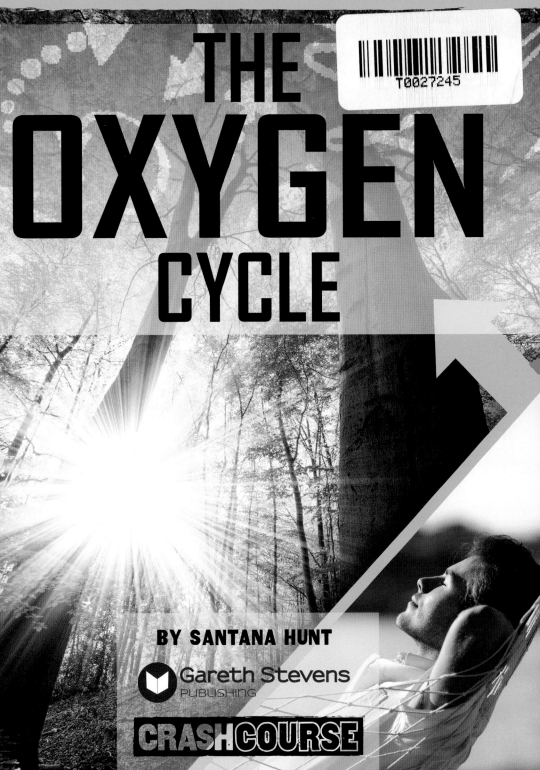

# A LOOK AT NATURE'S CYCLES

# THE OXYGEN CYCLE

BY SANTANA HUNT

Gareth Stevens
PUBLISHING

CRASHCOURSE

**Please visit our website, www.garethstevens.com. For a free color catalog of all our high-quality books, call toll free 1-800-542-2595 or fax 1-877-542-2596.**

**Library of Congress Cataloging-in-Publication Data**

Names: Hunt, Santana, author.
Title: The oxygen cycle / Santana Hunt.
Description: New York : Gareth Stevens Publishing, 2020. | Series: A look at
  nature's cycles | Includes bibliographical references and index.
Identifiers: LCCN 2018048719| ISBN 9781538241189 (pbk.) | ISBN 9781538241202
  (library bound) | ISBN 9781538241196 (6 pack)
Subjects: LCSH: Oxygen--Juvenile literature. | Atmospheric
  chemistry--Juvenile literature.
Classification: LCC QD181.O1 H846 2020 | DDC 551.51/12--dc23
LC record available at https://lccn.loc.gov/2018048719

First Edition

Published in 2020 by
**Gareth Stevens Publishing**
111 East 14th Street, Suite 349
New York, NY 10003

Designer: Sarah Liddell
Editor: Kristen Nelson

Photo credits: Cover, p. 1 (main) Guenter Albers/Shutterstock.com; cover, p. 1 (inset) Antonio Guillem/Shutterstock.com; arrow background used throughout Inka1/Shutterstock.com; p. 5 Akira Kaelyn/Shutterstock.com; p. 7 Materialscientist/Wikimedia Commons; p. 9 PRASANNAPIX/Shutterstock.com; p. 11 De Agostini Picture Library/Contributor/ De Agostini/Getty Images; p. 13 BlueRingMedia/Shutterstock.com; p. 15 Oleg Nesterov/ Shutterstock.com; p. 17 Sakurra/Shutterstock.com; p. 19 Vecton/Shutterstock.com; p. 21 Vibrant Image Studio/Shutterstock.com; p. 23 shooarts/Shutterstock.com; p. 25 Alessandro Zappalorto/Shutterstock.com; p. 27 Dudarev Mikhail/Shutterstock.com; p. 29 abcphotosystem/Shutterstock.com; p. 30 Designua/Shutterstock.com.

Printed in the United States of America

CPSIA compliance information: Batch #CS19GS: For further information contact Gareth Stevens, New York, New York at 1-800-542-2595.

# CONTENTS

Words in the glossary appear in **bold** type the first time they are used in the text.

# OXYGEN ON EARTH

Nearly all life on Earth depends on oxygen being present. It's part of the human body, in all bodies of water, and an important part of the **atmosphere**. We breathe it in, too! Oxygen's movement through its different forms in nature is called the oxygen cycle.

# MAKE THE GRADE

Oxygen makes up 21 percent of Earth's atmosphere.

5

Oxygen is an element that easily combines with most other elements. It can be present in **compounds** that are solid, liquid, or gas. When it's a gas, oxygen doesn't smell, have a taste, or have a color!

# MAKE THE GRADE

When oxygen combines with other elements, those elements have been "oxidized."

LIQUID OXYGEN

# START WITH PLANTS

The oxygen cycle most often includes the movement of breathable oxygen as it moves through plants and animals. It begins with the **process** of photosynthesis. This is the process by which most green plants and **algae** make their own food.

# MAKE THE GRADE

When oxygen is a gas, it's found as $O_2$ and $O_3$. $O_2$ is the gas used by plants and animals. $O_3$ is the oxygen found in the highest parts of Earth's atmosphere.

$O_2$

$O_3$

O

O

O

O

O

O = OXYGEN

First, these **organisms** take in light from the sun. A special green **pigment** found in some plant cells called chlorophyll allows them to use this energy in photosynthesis. Plants take in water and the gas carbon dioxide as well.

PLANT CELLS

CHLOROPLAST

# MAKE THE GRADE

Chlorophyll is in all green plants and mostly found in their leaves. It's found in cell parts called chloroplasts.

The sun's energy causes **chemical reactions** between carbon dioxide and water. The reactions form glucose, the sugar plants and algae break down for energy. Oxygen is a waste product of the reaction. It's given off into the air.

# MAKE THE GRADE

Plants do use some oxygen for their own life processes, but most leaves as waste.

SUNLIGHT

OXYGEN

CARBON DIOXIDE

SUGARS

WATER

# TO ANIMAL CELLS!

The second main part of the oxygen cycle is cellular respiration. When it includes an exchange of the gases oxygen and carbon dioxide, it's called aerobic respiration. In mammals like humans, oxygen is most often breathed in through the nose and mouth.

GILLS

# MAKE THE GRADE

Insects take in oxygen through spiracles, or holes in their body.
Fish use their gills or may take in oxygen through their skin!

In many animals, oxygen moves through the body to the lungs. There, it's exchanged for carbon dioxide. The animal breathes this out as a waste product of respiration. The body uses the oxygen to break down and use the energy taken in from food.

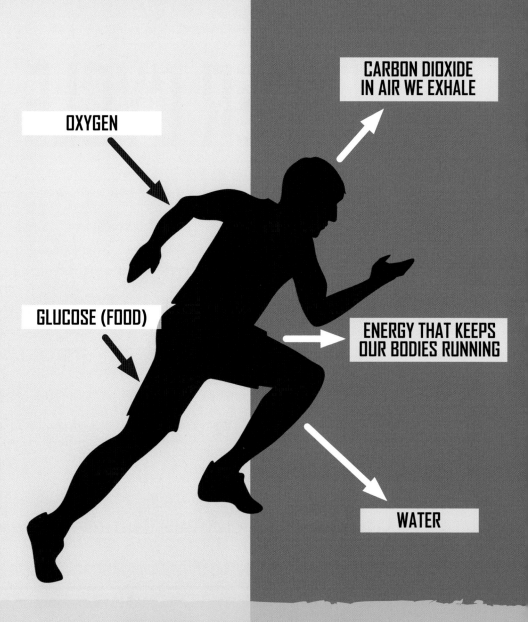

OXYGEN

CARBON DIOXIDE
IN AIR WE EXHALE

GLUCOSE (FOOD)

ENERGY THAT KEEPS
OUR BODIES RUNNING

WATER

# MAKE THE GRADE
The process of decay, or breaking down, of dead organisms
can also use oxygen and produce carbon dioxide.

# ANOTHER CYCLE

The oxygen cycle is linked to another of Earth's important cycles: the carbon cycle. This cycle tracks the movement of carbon through its different forms in nature. Carbon is an element found in all living things.

# MAKE THE GRADE

Carbon moves from one organism to another as animals give off carbon dioxide as waste and plants take it in. Some animals eat plants and take in carbon from their **tissues**.

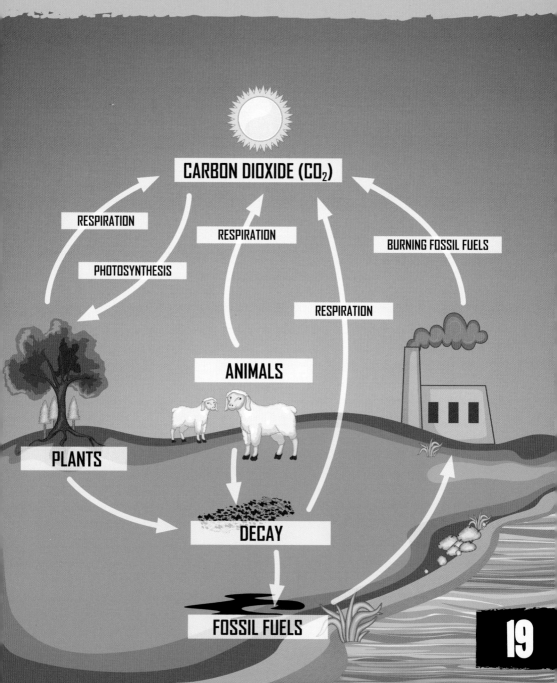

CARBON DIOXIDE (CO₂)

RESPIRATION

RESPIRATION

BURNING FOSSIL FUELS

PHOTOSYNTHESIS

RESPIRATION

ANIMALS

PLANTS

DECAY

FOSSIL FUELS

Photosynthesis gives off billions of tons of oxygen into the air each year. Animals and other organisms take in about that amount and give off carbon dioxide in exchange. So, the oxygen and carbon cycles work together!

# MAKE THE GRADE

Oxygen can become part of the atmosphere by a process called photolysis. A certain kind of **radiation** can break down water within the atmosphere and free the oxygen from water **molecules**.

21

# NOT ALL AIR

Oxygen is one of the most plentiful elements on Earth, but most of it isn't found in the atmosphere or the air people breathe. About 99.5 percent is found in the lithosphere, the outermost part of Earth! This stored oxygen can become part of the main oxygen cycle.

# MAKE THE GRADE

Together, Earth's crust and upper mantle
are called the lithosphere.

CRUST

UPPER MANTLE

MANTLE

OUTER CORE

INNER CORE

Because oxygen combines with other elements easily, it's found in many kinds of rock that are part of Earth's crust. As rocks face weathering—or the wearing away by wind, water, and the activities of living things—they can break down. Oxygen may be given off!

# MAKE THE GRADE

Some sea creatures make shells out of calcium carbonate, matter that has lots of oxygen in it. After these creatures die, their shells may become part of the lithosphere as limestone.

# FOSSIL FUEL EFFECT

The burning of fossil fuels adds carbon dioxide and harmful gases into Earth's atmosphere. However, the amount of oxygen in the atmosphere is only decreasing slightly as plants continue to use carbon dioxide and produce oxygen. Still, the use of fossil fuels harms Earth in many other ways.

# MAKE THE GRADE

Fossil fuels are the long-buried remains of plants and animals that can be burned for their energy.

27

# WITHOUT OXYGEN

The oxygen cycle is very important to life on Earth. Without oxygen to breathe, animals would die out. And without animals breathing out carbon dioxide, plants would die out! The parts of the cycle work together to keep Earth healthy and full of life.

# MAKE THE GRADE

Algae—not plants—replace about 90 percent
of the oxygen used on Earth.

ALGAE

# THE OXYGEN CYCLE

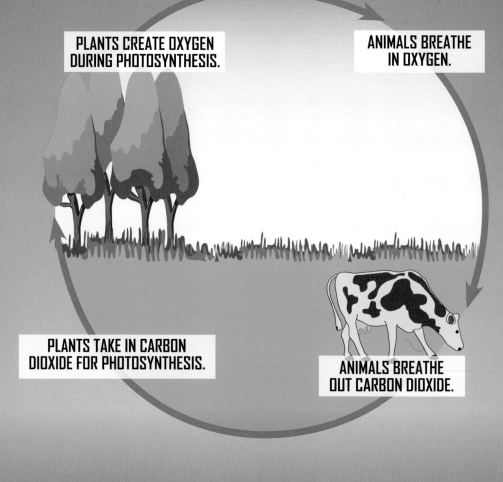

PLANTS CREATE OXYGEN DURING PHOTOSYNTHESIS.

ANIMALS BREATHE IN OXYGEN.

PLANTS TAKE IN CARBON DIOXIDE FOR PHOTOSYNTHESIS.

ANIMALS BREATHE OUT CARBON DIOXIDE.

# GLOSSARY

**algae:** plantlike living things that are mostly found in water

**atmosphere:** the mixture of gases that surround a planet

**chemical reaction:** the mixing of matter with other matter and the change this causes

**compound:** two or more unlike atoms joined together

**molecule:** a very small piece of matter

**organism:** a living thing

**pigment:** a substance that gives a plant or animal color

**process:** a series of steps or actions taken to complete something

**radiation:** waves of energy

**tissue:** matter that forms the parts of living things

# FOR MORE INFORMATION

## BOOKS

Conklin, Wendy. *Earth's Cycles*. Huntington Beach, CA: Teacher Created Materials, 2016.

Hurt, Avery Elizabeth. *Oxygen*. New York, NY: Enslow Publishing, LLC, 2019.

## WEBSITES

### Ecosystem: The Oxygen Cycle
*www.ducksters.com/science/ecosystems/oxygen_cycle.php*
Review the oxygen cycle on this website for kids.

### Photosynthesis for Kids Video
*easyscienceforkids.com/photosynthesis-for-kids-video*
Watch a video and learn even more about photosynthesis.

# INDEX